THE NEXT PRESIDENT WILL DO THE SAME

KING ZOLA

Table of Contents

INTRODUCTION

In the realm of politics, we are constantly bombarded with promises of change, hope, and a better future. With each new election cycle, candidates emerge, rallying the public with their grand visions and lofty commitments. The electorate, weary of the status quo and yearning for progress, eagerly embraces these promises, hoping that the next president will be the catalyst for real transformation.

However, time and again, we find ourselves disillusioned. As the dust settles and the campaign fervor subsides, it becomes clear that the next president will do the same. The cycle repeats as if trapped in a perpetual loop of unfulfilled expectations. But why does this happen? What are the underlying forces that contribute to this seemingly never-ending cycle of broken promises and unmet aspirations?

In this book, titled "The Next President Will Do the Same," we embark on a journey to uncover the truths behind this phenomenon. Through an exploration of historical precedents, systemic flaws, and the impact of various stakeholders, we aim to shed light on the factors that perpetuate the status quo. By dissecting the complexities of politics, we seek to understand why change is elusive and why our hopes for a transformative leader often go unfulfilled.

Chapter 1: "The Illusion of Change" examines the allure of campaign promises and the disillusionment that follows. We delve into the historical context, examining notable instances where politicians made grandiose pledges only to fall short of their commitments. Through this exploration, we gain insight into the patterns and pitfalls of political rhetoric, understanding how it can captivate and deceive.

Chapter 2: "The Influence of Special Interests" exposes the role of lobbying and corporate interests in shaping political agendas. We delve into the murky world of money in politics, uncovering the influence of campaign financing and the revolving door between government and the private sector. By understanding the power of special interests, we can better comprehend why systemic change often eludes us.

In Chapter 3: "The Constraints of the Political System," we navigate the complexities of governance and the roadblocks to progress. Partisan politics, gridlock, and the intricate system of checks and balances all contribute to the inertia that hinders transformative action. Through analysis and case studies, we reveal the challenges faced by politicians as they navigate the intricate web of the political system.

Chapter 4: "The Inertia of Institutionalism" shines a light on the resistance to change within government institutions. Bureaucracies, entrenched in their ways, often impede reform and perpetuate policies from administration to administration. By examining real-world examples, we unravel the layers of institutional inertia, gaining a deeper understanding of the forces that resist change.

"The Impact of Global Forces" is the focus of Chapter 5. We explore how international politics and economics shape the decisions made by our leaders. Global commitments, geopolitical considerations, and the delicate balance between national interests and global responsibilities all influence the actions of our elected officials. Understanding these factors is crucial in comprehending why change is often tempered by external forces.

In Chapter 6: "The Role of Public Opinion," we investigate the limitations of public sentiment in shaping policy. We examine the manipulation of public opinion, the influence of media and social media, and the challenges faced by leaders in governing a society with diverse and sometimes conflicting viewpoints. By unraveling the complexities of public opinion, we gain insight into the constraints faced by politicians.

 explores potential solutions to break the cycle of stagnation. We examine alternative political systems, proposals for campaign finance reform, and the need for institutional change. By exploring grassroots movements and their potential for impact, we uncover avenues for transforming the political landscape.

 we draw on the lessons learned throughout

 the book to paint a picture of possibility. We examine historical examples of transformation and analyze the power of an engaged and informed citizenry. By understanding the opportunities for systemic change and the importance of holding politicians accountable, we cultivate a sense of optimism for a future that breaks free from the confines of the recurring cycle.

As we embark on this exploration of political dynamics, it is essential to approach the subject matter with an open mind and a critical eye. By understanding the underlying forces that contribute to the perpetuation of the status quo, we can begin to question and challenge the existing system. Through knowledge and awareness, we can empower ourselves to demand genuine change from our leaders, breaking free from the cycle of empty promises and unfulfilled potential. Together, let us embark on this journey, seeking a deeper understanding of why the next president will do the same.

Chapter 1

THE ILLUSION OF CHANGE

Introduction

In the realm of politics, the allure of change is a powerful force. It captivates the hearts and minds of the electorate, offering a glimmer of hope for a better future. During election seasons, politicians master the art of rhetoric, crafting promises that tap into our deepest desires and aspirations. They paint vivid pictures of transformation, assuring us that if we elect them, they will usher in a new era of progress and prosperity.

However, as the fervor of the campaign trail subsides and the realities of governance take hold, we often find ourselves facing the stark reality of unfulfilled promises. The illusion of change begins to dissipate, replaced by a sense of disillusionment. It seems as though no matter who takes office, the cycle repeats itself, leaving us wondering why our hopes for transformation are so often shattered.

Deconstructing Political Promises

To understand the illusion of change, we must first deconstruct the nature of political promises. Campaign rhetoric, carefully crafted to resonate with voters, often relies on lofty ideals and sweeping visions. Politicians make commitments to tackle pressing issues, from healthcare reform to economic revitalization, promising a brighter future for all. These promises, delivered with conviction and charm, create a sense of anticipation among the electorate.

Historical Precedents

Examining historical precedents reveals a pattern of broken promises. Throughout the annals of politics, we can find numerous examples where leaders, once elected, failed to deliver on their commitments. Whether it is a failure to pass comprehensive legislation or a departure from campaign positions, the track record of unfulfilled promises is disheartening. From presidential campaigns to local elections, the pattern persists across different levels of government.

The Role of Media

The media plays a significant role in perpetuating the illusion of change. During election cycles, candidates receive immense coverage and attention, providing them with a platform to promote their promises. However, once in office, the media often shifts its focus elsewhere, leaving little room for scrutiny and holding leaders accountable for their commitments. The lack of continuous media scrutiny contributes to the perpetuation of the illusion, allowing politicians to escape scrutiny and accountability.

The Emotional Appeal

The illusion of change is not solely a result of empty promises; it also stems from the emotional appeal of campaign rhetoric. Politicians tap into the fears, frustrations, and hopes of the electorate, creating an emotional connection that resonates deeply. By invoking powerful imagery and using persuasive language, they generate a sense of unity and purpose, convincing us that they are the harbinger of change.

The Pitfalls of Overpromising

One of the main reasons for the perpetuation of the illusion of change is the tendency of politicians to overpromise. In the quest for votes, candidates may make unrealistic commitments or downplay the complexities of governance. They offer quick fixes and simple solutions to complex problems, creating an atmosphere of unrealistic expectations.

When these promises inevitably fall short, disillusionment sets in.

Managing Expectations

It is crucial for both politicians and the electorate to manage expectations realistically. Politicians must be transparent about the challenges they face in implementing their proposed changes, while voters need to be discerning and critical when evaluating campaign promises. By fostering a culture of informed skepticism, we can mitigate the impact of the illusion of change and hold politicians accountable for their actions.

Conclusion

Chapter 1 exposes the illusion of change that permeates our political landscape. By deconstructing political promises, examining historical precedents, and understanding the role of media and emotional appeal, we gain insight into the mechanisms that perpetuate this illusion. Recognizing the pitfalls of overpromising and managing our expectations are essential steps in navigating the complexities of the political landscape. In the following chapters, we will continue to unravel the forces

 that contribute to the cycle of unfulfilled promises, providing a comprehensive understanding of why the next president will do the same.

Chapter 2

THE INFLUENCE OF SPECIAL INTERESTS

Introduction

In the realm of politics, the influence of special interests has become a pervasive and potent force. Lobbying groups, corporate entities, and other powerful stakeholders exert significant sway over political decision-making processes. Their interests and agendas often shape policy outcomes, leaving the electorate wondering if the next president will truly bring about change or succumb to the pressures of these influential entities. In this chapter, we delve into the intricate web of special interest influence, exploring the extent to which it impacts our political system.

The Power of Lobbying

Lobbying is a cornerstone of special interest influence in politics. Corporations, advocacy groups, and professional lobbyists employ various strategies to advance their interests and secure favorable outcomes. They engage in direct persuasion, leverage financial contributions, and utilize their access to policymakers to shape legislation and regulations. The vast resources at their disposal enable them to effectively amplify their voices and exert considerable pressure on elected officials.

Campaign Financing

Money plays a central role in politics, and campaign financing has a profound impact on the decisions made by politicians. Special interest groups contribute significant sums of money to political campaigns, effectively influencing the electoral process. Donations and financial support often come with expectations of favorable treatment, creating a potential conflict of interest for elected officials. The need to secure funds for reelection can drive politicians to align their policies and actions with the wishes of their financial supporters.

The Revolving Door

The revolving door between the government and the private sector further amplifies the influence of special interests. Individuals who have served in public office often transition to lucrative positions in industries they once regulated. This revolving door creates a symbiotic relationship between policymakers and corporate interests, blurring the lines between public service and private gain. The potential for conflicts of interest and the risk of regulatory capture loom large, raising concerns about impartial decision-making.

Case Studies

Examining specific case studies allows us to grasp the magnitude of special interest influence on policy outcomes. We delve into examples where powerful lobbying groups and corporate interests have successfully shaped legislation in their favor. From the energy and healthcare sectors to finance and telecommunications, we uncover instances where policy decisions align closely with the interests of influential entities. These case studies provide tangible evidence of how special interests can shape the political landscape.

Public Perception and Accountability

The influence of special interests raises questions about the accountability of elected officials. When politicians prioritize the demands of powerful stakeholders over the interests of the general public, the democratic process is compromised. The public's perception of government efficacy and trust in political institutions can be eroded. It is essential to foster transparency, ethics, and robust regulations that mitigate the undue influence of special interests, ensuring that the voice of the people remains at the core of decision-making processes.

Reform and Checks

Addressing the influence of special interests necessitates reform efforts aimed at restoring the integrity of the political system. Campaign finance reform, stricter lobbying regulations, and transparency measures are potential avenues to limit the undue influence of special interests. Furthermore, implementing effective checks and balances, along with independent oversight mechanisms, can help safeguard against the subversion of public interest by powerful entities.

Conclusion

Chapter 2 exposes the pervasive influence of special interests on our political system. By examining the power of lobbying, the impact of campaign financing, and the revolving door between government and the private sector, we gain a comprehensive understanding of the mechanisms through which special interests shape policy outcomes. The case studies provided highlight the tangible effects of this influence. To safeguard the integrity of our democratic processes, it is crucial to address the sway of special interests through reform and accountability measures. In the following chapters, we will continue to explore the factors that contribute to the perpetuation of the status quo, shedding light on why the next president will do the same.

THE CONSTRAINTS OF THE POLITICAL SYSTEM

Introduction

The political system within which leaders operate plays a significant role in shaping their ability to enact meaningful change. While politicians may enter office with grand visions and promises, they are often confronted with a complex web of constraints that hinder their capacity to deliver on those commitments. In this chapter, we delve into the inherent limitations and challenges of the political system, exploring how partisan politics, gridlock, and the system of checks and balances impede transformative action.

Partisan Politics

Partisan politics, characterized by deeply entrenched divisions along ideological lines, poses a significant obstacle to progress. The adversarial nature of politics often leads to a focus on scoring political points rather than finding common ground and implementing effective solutions. The polarization between political parties can result in gridlock and a lack of bipartisan cooperation, impeding the passage of legislation and hindering the pursuit of transformative policies.

Gridlock and Stalemate

Gridlock occurs when the political system is deadlocked and unable to move forward due to the absence of consensus. Divisions among politicians, both within and between parties, can lead to legislative stalemates. The inability to find compromise and reach agreements can paralyze the decision-making process and prevent the realization of meaningful change. Gridlock is often exacerbated by factors such as party loyalty, ideological rigidity, and the influence of special interests.

Checks and Balances

The system of checks and balances, designed to prevent the abuse of power and maintain a separation of powers, can also impede swift and decisive action. While intended as a safeguard, it can create a complex web of processes and approvals that slow down decision-making. The requirement for multiple branches of government to collaborate and obtain consensus can lead to compromises that dilute the original vision and hinder transformative reforms.

Institutional Inertia

Government institutions, characterized by bureaucracies and established protocols, often exhibit resistance to change. Entrenched bureaucracies may be resistant to new ideas and resistant to the disruption of established routines. The inertia of these institutions can make it challenging for politicians to implement their proposed changes effectively. The complexities of navigating these bureaucracies and overcoming institutional resistance can contribute to the perpetuation of the status quo.

Case Studies

Examining specific case studies allows us to understand how the constraints of the political system manifest in real-world scenarios. We explore instances where partisan politics, gridlock, and checks and balances have impeded transformative action. Through these case studies, we gain insight into the challenges faced by politicians in navigating the intricacies of the political system.

Navigating the Constraints

While the constraints of the political system can be formidable, there are strategies and approaches that politicians can employ to navigate them effectively. Building coalitions, fostering relationships across party lines, and prioritizing issue-based cooperation can help overcome the barriers of partisan politics. Seeking common ground and engaging in inclusive decision-making processes can also alleviate gridlock. Additionally, understanding and working within the established systems of checks and balances can help navigate the complexities and ensure compliance with democratic norms.

Conclusion

Chapter 3 sheds light on the inherent constraints of the political system that hinder transformative action. Partisan politics, gridlock, the system of checks and balances, and institutional inertia collectively pose significant challenges for politicians seeking to enact change.

By examining case studies and exploring strategies for navigating these constraints, we gain a deeper understanding of the complexities faced by leaders. In the subsequent chapters, we will continue to explore the forces that contribute to the perpetuation of the status quo, unraveling why the next president will do the same.

Chapter 4

THE INERTIA OF INSTITUTIONALISM

Introduction

Institutions are the backbone of any political system, providing structure, stability, and continuity. However, the inertia of institutionalism can often become a barrier to meaningful change. In this chapter, we explore how the established norms, bureaucracies, and vested interests within institutions can contribute to the perpetuation of the status quo. We examine the challenges faced by politicians in navigating institutional inertia and discuss potential strategies for overcoming these barriers.

The Power of Tradition

Tradition and established practices within institutions can exert a powerful influence on decision-making processes. Long-standing norms and customs shape the expectations of stakeholders, making it difficult for politicians to deviate from the established path. The resistance to change fueled by the desire to maintain stability and uphold tradition can stifle innovative ideas and limit the potential for transformative action.

Bureaucratic Resistance

Bureaucracies, with their hierarchies, procedures, and standard operating protocols, can be resistant to change. The established routines and entrenched structures within bureaucracies can hinder the implementation of new policies and initiatives. Bureaucrats, tasked with ensuring stability and adherence to established processes, may exhibit a natural inclination to maintain the status quo, leading to inertia and resistance to transformative action.

Vested Interests

Institutions often have vested interests that seek to protect their influence and power. These interests can manifest in the form of lobbying groups, influential stakeholders, and internal factions within the institutions themselves. The resistance to change from these vested interests can create barriers for politicians seeking to enact transformative policies. These interests may seek to preserve their privileged positions and resist reforms that could challenge their status quo.

Cultural Norms and Beliefs

Cultural norms and beliefs, deeply ingrained within society, can also contribute to institutional inertia. Societal expectations, values, and ingrained biases shape the way institutions function and influence decision-making processes. Challenging cultural norms can be met with resistance, as they represent deeply held beliefs and traditions that may be difficult to overcome. Overcoming these cultural barriers requires a broader societal shift and a change in collective attitudes towards transformative change.

Strategies for Overcoming Institutional Inertia

While institutional inertia can be a formidable obstacle, there are strategies that politicians can employ to overcome these barriers:

- **Building Coalitions:** Creating alliances and partnerships with like-minded individuals and groups within institutions can help garner support for transformative action and increase the chances of success.

- **Engaging Stakeholders:** Involving stakeholders in the decision-making process and seeking their input can help build consensus and overcome resistance to change.

- **Incremental Change:** Breaking down transformative goals into smaller, more manageable steps can make them more palatable to institutions and ease resistance to change.

- **Leadership and Vision:** Strong leadership, combined with a clear vision for change, can inspire others within institutions and mobilize support for transformative action.

- **Public Pressure:**
  Harnessing public support and mobilizing public opinion can create external pressure on institutions, compelling them to embrace change.

Conclusion:

Chapter 4 highlights the inertia of institutionalism as a significant barrier to transformative change. The power of tradition, bureaucratic resistance, vested interests, and cultural norms all contribute to the perpetuation of the status quo. Understanding these challenges and employing strategies to overcome institutional inertia are crucial for politicians seeking to bring about meaningful change. In the subsequent chapters, we will continue to explore the factors that contribute to the recurring

cycle of unfulfilled promises, shedding
light on why the next president will do
the same.

Chapter 5

THE IMPACT OF GLOBAL FORCES

Introduction

In an increasingly interconnected world, the actions and decisions of political leaders are not isolated within national borders. Global forces exert significant influence on domestic policies and shape the ability of the next president to bring about substantial change. In this chapter, we explore the impact of global forces such as globalization, international relations, and economic interdependence on the political landscape. We examine how these forces can limit the scope of transformative action and contribute to the repetition of familiar patterns.

Globalization and Interconnectedness

Globalization has facilitated the integration of economies, cultures, and societies, transcending national boundaries. The interconnectedness brought about by globalization has both positive and negative implications for political leaders. While it offers opportunities for cooperation, trade, and innovation, it also subjects governments to external pressures and constraints. The need to navigate global dynamics and adhere to international norms can limit the autonomy and flexibility of political leaders in pursuing transformative policies.

International Relations and Diplomacy

The complex web of international relations and diplomatic considerations can impact the actions of political leaders. Engaging with other nations requires a delicate balancing act, as decisions must consider not only domestic interests but also the broader global context. Negotiating agreements, navigating diplomatic tensions, and adhering to international obligations can often limit the ability of leaders to enact transformative policies that deviate from established norms and expectations.

Economic Interdependence

In an era of economic interdependence, the actions of political leaders are closely tied to global economic realities. Trade agreements, financial systems, and multinational corporations exert significant influence on domestic policies. The need to maintain economic stability, attract foreign investment, and navigate global economic fluctuations can limit the scope of transformative action. The intricate web of economic interdependence can create constraints and dependencies that restrict the ability to bring about substantial change.

Power Dynamics and Global Influence

Global power dynamics play a crucial role in shaping the actions and decisions of political leaders. Major powers, regional alliances, and influential international organizations wield considerable influence over policy outcomes. The pursuit of national interests often intersects with geopolitical considerations, and political leaders must navigate these power dynamics to ensure their actions align with strategic objectives. The dominance of powerful nations and the influence they exert can constrain the transformative potential of leaders.

Multilateralism and Collective Action

Addressing global challenges, such as climate change, requires collective action and multilateral cooperation. Political leaders must navigate the complexities of international negotiations and seek consensus among diverse nations with competing interests. The need to align with global agreements and mobilize collective action can limit the ability to pursue transformative policies independently. Balancing national priorities with the imperatives of global cooperation becomes a delicate task for political leaders.

Strategies for Navigating Global Forces

Despite the constraints imposed by global forces, political leaders can employ strategies to effectively navigate these dynamics:

- **Diplomatic Engagement:** Active

engagement in international forums and diplomatic efforts can help shape global narratives and align international priorities with domestic transformative goals.

- **Strategic Alliances:** Forming strategic alliances and partnerships with like-minded nations and international organizations can amplify the impact of transformative policies and create momentum for change.

- **Global Advocacy:** Leveraging platforms and networks to advocate for global reforms and mobilize support for transformative action can increase the chances of success.

- **Balancing National Interests:** Striking a balance between national interests and global responsibilities is essential. Political leaders must navigate global forces while safeguarding domestic priorities and ensuring the well-being of their citizens.

Conclusion

Chapter 5 highlights the impact of global forces on the ability of political leaders to bring about transformative change. Globalization, international relations, economic interdependence, power dynamics, and multilateralism all shape the political landscape. Understanding and effectively navigating these global forces are crucial for leaders seeking to make a substantial impact. In the subsequent chapters, we will continue to explore the factors that contribute to the perpetuation of the status quo, unraveling why the next president will do the same.

Chapter 6

THE ROLE OF PUBLIC OPINION

Introduction

Public opinion holds significant influence over the actions and decisions of political leaders. The sentiments, beliefs, and preferences of the general population shape the political landscape and can either propel or hinder transformative change. In this chapter, we explore the role of public opinion in shaping the behavior of politicians and delve into the factors that influence public perception. By understanding the dynamics of public opinion, we can gain insights into why the next president may face challenges in breaking the cycle of the status quo.

The Power of Public Perception

Public opinion serves as a barometer of societal attitudes and values. The support, or lack thereof, from the public can have a profound impact on the actions and decisions of political leaders. Leaders often seek to align their policies with public sentiment to maintain popular support and ensure reelection. The influence of public opinion can shape the priorities of political leaders and constrain their ability to enact transformative policies that may deviate from prevailing public sentiment.

Media and Information Landscape

The media plays a crucial role in shaping public opinion. News outlets, social media platforms, and other forms of media influence public perception by framing issues, highlighting certain narratives, and selectively reporting on events. The media landscape and the spread of information can impact the level of public awareness, understanding, and engagement on critical issues. The biases and sensationalism within media outlets can shape public opinion and contribute to the perpetuation of the status quo.

Political Messaging and Persuasion

Political leaders employ messaging strategies to shape public opinion and garner support for their agendas. Effective communication and persuasion techniques are utilized to influence public perceptions of policies and initiatives. The framing of issues, emotional appeals, and the presentation of compelling narratives all play a role in shaping public opinion. However, political messaging can also perpetuate the status quo by reinforcing existing beliefs and preferences rather than challenging them.

Public Engagement and Activism

Public engagement and activism can drive transformative change by mobilizing public opinion and putting pressure on political leaders. Grassroots movements, protests, and citizen activism have the potential to shape the political discourse and influence policy outcomes. However, the success of public engagement efforts depends on various factors, including the level of organization, coordination, and the ability to sustain momentum over time.

Complexity and Limited Understanding

Public opinion is also influenced by the complexity of political issues and the limited understanding of their intricacies. Many policy challenges require nuanced solutions that may not be easily comprehensible to the general public. The complexity of these issues can create challenges in garnering public support for transformative policies that necessitate significant changes or tradeoffs. Simplistic or misleading narratives may dominate public discourse, hindering the potential for informed and constructive discussions.

Changing Public Opinion

Public opinion is not fixed and can evolve over time. Shifts in societal attitudes, generational changes, and transformative events can reshape public sentiment. Political leaders have the opportunity to shape public opinion through effective communication, education, and transparency. By actively engaging with the public, leaders can foster a deeper understanding of complex issues and influence public perceptions in favor of transformative change.

Conclusion

Chapter 6 emphasizes the pivotal role of public opinion in shaping the behavior of political leaders. The media landscape, political messaging, public engagement, and the limited understanding of complex issues all contribute to the dynamics of public opinion. Understanding the influence of public sentiment is crucial for political leaders seeking to bring about transformative change. In the subsequent chapters, we will continue to explore the forces that contribute to the perpetuation of the status quo, shedding light on why the next president will do the same.

Chapter 7

ALTERNATIVES AND REFORM

Introduction

While the previous chapters have outlined the various factors that contribute to the repetition of familiar patterns in politics, this chapter explores the possibilities for change and reform. Despite the challenges and constraints faced by political leaders, alternative approaches and reform initiatives offer opportunities to break free from the cycle of the status quo. In this chapter, we examine potential alternatives and avenues for transformative action, focusing on innovative strategies, grassroots movements, and systemic reforms.

Innovative Strategies

Innovation and creative thinking can offer new pathways for political leaders to effect change. Embracing innovative strategies such as technology-driven solutions, data-driven policymaking, and evidence-based approaches can enhance the effectiveness of policies and increase their transformative potential. Harnessing the power of innovation and adopting forward-thinking practices can lead to novel solutions that address complex societal challenges.

Grassroots Movements and Citizen Empowerment

Grassroots movements have the power to shape the political landscape by mobilizing public opinion and demanding change from the ground up. These movements, driven by passionate citizens, can challenge the status quo and advocate for transformative policies. By empowering citizens, fostering civic engagement, and amplifying marginalized voices, political leaders can harness the collective power of the people and foster a more inclusive and participatory democracy.

Systemic Reforms

Addressing the root causes of the perpetuation of the status quo requires systemic reforms. Structural changes to political institutions, electoral systems, campaign finance regulations, and governance mechanisms can help mitigate the constraints that hinder transformative action. By promoting transparency, accountability, and democratic values, systemic reforms can create a more conducive environment for political leaders to implement transformative policies and break free from established norms.

Policy Innovation and Experimentation

Experimenting with policy approaches and piloting initiatives on a smaller scale can provide valuable insights into the viability and impact of transformative policies. Political leaders can embrace policy innovation by creating spaces for experimentation, establishing policy labs, and encouraging evidence-based evaluations of pilot projects. By embracing a culture of learning and adaptability, leaders can identify effective approaches and overcome resistance to change.

Collaborative Governance

Collaborative governance, characterized by partnerships between government, civil society, and the private sector, offers a pathway for transformative action. By fostering collaborative relationships, political leaders can tap into the expertise, resources, and diverse perspectives of different stakeholders. Collaborative governance models promote inclusive decision-making processes, facilitate consensus-building, and create ownership of transformative policies, leading to more sustainable and impactful outcomes.

International Cooperation and Learning

Political leaders can also look beyond national borders and engage in international cooperation and learning. By exchanging best practices, sharing knowledge, and collaborating with other nations, leaders can gain insights into successful transformative approaches and adapt them to their own contexts. International cooperation can help overcome challenges posed by global forces and foster collective action towards shared goals.

Conclusion

Chapter 7 explores alternatives and avenues for reform that can break the cycle of the status quo. Innovative strategies, grassroots movements, systemic reforms, policy experimentation, collaborative governance, and international cooperation all offer opportunities for transformative action. By embracing these alternatives and implementing meaningful reforms, political leaders can navigate the constraints outlined in previous chapters and pave the way for a new era of progressive change. In the subsequent chapters, we will consolidate our understanding of the forces at play and draw conclusions about why the next president may or may not be able to break free from the cycle of repetition.

Chapter 8

HOPE FOR CHANGE?

Introduction

After exploring the various factors that contribute to the repetition of patterns in politics and examining potential alternatives and avenues for reform, this chapter delves into the question of whether there is hope for real change. Is it possible for the next president to break free from the cycle of the status quo and bring about transformative action? In this chapter, we evaluate the prospects for change, considering the complexities, challenges, and potential catalysts that could lead to a departure from familiar patterns.

The Complexities of Change

Bringing about meaningful change is a complex task that requires navigating numerous interrelated factors. Political, economic, social, and cultural dynamics all play a role in shaping the possibilities for transformative action. The intricate web of interconnected challenges can make it difficult to dismantle the status quo and implement substantial reforms. However, recognizing the complexities is the first step toward developing a comprehensive strategy for change.

The Role of Leadership

Leadership plays a pivotal role in driving change. The next president's vision, values, and ability to inspire and mobilize others will significantly influence the prospects for transformative action. Effective leadership entails making difficult decisions, confronting vested interests, and taking risks to challenge the status quo. Leaders who possess the courage, determination, and strategic acumen to navigate obstacles can create an environment conducive to change.

Catalysts for Change

Certain catalysts can spur transformative action and provide opportunities for change. Crises, whether economic, social, or environmental, can serve as wake-up calls that demand a departure from business as usual. These crises often expose vulnerabilities, galvanize public opinion, and create a sense of urgency for transformative action. Additionally, shifts in societal attitudes, demographic changes, and technological advancements can also act as catalysts, propelling the need for change.

Public Demand and Mobilization

The power of public demand and mobilization should not be underestimated. When citizens actively engage in the political process, voice their concerns, and demand change, political leaders are more likely to respond. Grassroots movements, social activism, and public pressure can shape the agenda, influence policy decisions, and hold leaders accountable. The collective voice of the people has the potential to push for transformative action and disrupt the cycle of the status quo.

Overcoming Resistance and Pushback

Resistance to change is inevitable, particularly from entrenched interests that benefit from the existing system. Political leaders must anticipate and navigate resistance, developing strategies to overcome pushback and garner support for transformative policies. Building coalitions, engaging stakeholders, and effectively communicating the benefits of change can help neutralize opposition and rally support for progressive reforms.

Building Sustainable Momentum

Sustaining momentum for change is crucial for long-term success. Transformative action requires more than just short-term measures; it necessitates sustained commitment, resilience, and perseverance. Political leaders must foster a culture of continuity, ensuring that transformative policies are not abandoned or diluted over time. By building sustainable momentum, leaders can create lasting change and break free from the recurring cycle of unfulfilled promises.

Conclusion

Chapter 8 evaluates the prospects for change and reflects on the question of whether there is hope for the next president to bring about transformative action. While the complexities, challenges, and resistance to change are substantial, catalysts for change, effective leadership, public demand, and sustained momentum offer rays of hope. By understanding the dynamics at play, acknowledging the need for innovative approaches, and harnessing the power of collective action, there is a real possibility for the next president to break free from the cycle of the status quo and usher in an era of meaningful change. In the final chapter, we will draw conclusions based on our exploration and provide insights into the path forward.

CONCLUSION

Throughout this book, we have explored the dynamics that contribute to the repetition of familiar patterns in politics, shedding light on why the next president will likely continue in the same trajectory. We examined factors such as the illusion of change, the influence of special interests, the constraints of the political system, the inertia of institutionalism, the impact of global forces, the role of public opinion, and potential avenues for reform. While these factors create significant challenges and constraints, there are glimmers of hope for transformative action.

Change is a complex and multifaceted process that requires a comprehensive understanding of the forces at play. The next president must recognize the complexities and intricacies of the political landscape, acknowledging the interplay between various factors. By doing so, they can develop strategies that navigate constraints and capitalize on opportunities for change.

Effective leadership will be crucial in driving transformative action. Leaders must possess vision, courage, and strategic acumen to challenge the status quo, make difficult decisions, and mobilize others toward a common purpose. They must embrace innovative strategies, empower grassroots movements, and pursue systemic reforms that address the root causes of the perpetuation of the status quo.

Public opinion and citizen engagement also play a pivotal role. The voice of the people can shape the political discourse, demand change, and hold leaders accountable. By fostering a culture of active citizenship, leaders can harness the collective power of the public and create an environment where transformative policies can thrive.

Overcoming resistance and building sustainable momentum are vital for long-term success. Political leaders must anticipate and navigate pushback from vested interests, rallying support for progressive reforms. Sustaining momentum requires continuity, resilience, and a commitment to upholding transformative policies over time.

While the challenges are significant, there are catalysts for change that can provide opportunities for departure from the status quo. Crises, shifts in societal attitudes, technological advancements, and demographic changes can act as catalysts, demanding a reevaluation of established norms and practices.

In conclusion, the next president faces formidable challenges in breaking free from the cycle of repetition. However, by understanding the complexities, embracing innovative strategies, engaging with the public, and pursuing systemic reforms, there is hope for transformative action. It is through effective leadership, public demand, and sustained momentum that we can envision a future where the next president will not do the same but will instead pave the way for meaningful change, shaping a better and more progressive society for all.

ABOUT THE AUTHOR

EMAIL:
aarasheedmohammed@gmail.com

In this book, titled "The Next President Will Do the Same," we embark on a journey to uncover the truths behind this phenomenon. Through an exploration of historical precedents, systemic flaws, and the impact of various stakeholders, we aim to shed light on the factors that perpetuate the status quo. By dissecting the complexities of politics, we seek to understand why change is elusive and why our hopes for a transformative leader often go unfulfilled.

Alberto L. Wilson

THE PATH TO A HAPPIER LIFE

Making Simple Changes for Healthy Habits